Stray in the Matrix

Issam Raad

Stray in the Matrix

First Edition 2022
issamfnw@gmail.com

Cover design by Issam Raad.
Book design by Issam Raad.

Stray in the Matrix

This book is not a book; it's an idea. This idea is not an idea but rather a riddle. This riddle is not an unknown but rather a known one. This known is not a known, but rather a life. This life is not a life but rather a book. This book is everywhere, and everyone browses it. But it contains mysteries, and only the ones who want to understand will read it.

I dedicate this idea to my mother, father, family, and all who seek to understand.

Sincerely,
Issam Raad.

Index

Introduction

Stray in the matrix... The title may be more than a title. The cover page may be hiding something. The book may be holding riddles. Chapters may be more than chapters and maybe somehow relatable. Space and time may be ambiguous and maybe unreal. Characters may be part of a story, nothing more. Mistakes may be made on purpose... The beginning is the end, and the end is the beginning; Everything is connected.

"All that we see or seem is just a dream within a dream" — *Edgar Allan Poe.*

"Yes, it's quiet in here. No, keep the lights away; I can see it all..."

....

"Now? Why? A secret? But I can't see anything; it's so glaring outside... Till when? You won't say anything? Do I even have a choice?"

....

"Mm, well, I'll try..."

....

"Mama...

A Moment

...Not an outlaw, but a free man!"

"Do you mean that all those people are wrong, and you're here to guide them to the right path? The world is changing, and you must change with it. Wake up..."

"I never said that! Nobody's wrong; that's not the correct term. It's there's something intolerable about the world. I don't know how to explain it. I can feel it in my bones, tearing me apart and driving me mad!"

"There is some comfort in the emptiness of the sea; no past, no future." —The Last Samurai, 2003.

Childhood is innocent. We never really think of anything but having fun and filling our bellies. Magnificent how simple and peaceful it is. Our minds are so quiet, for we never interpret what we observe but believe it all and enjoy it. We are so happy because we only live in the 'now,' which alone is a blessing. Yet, life moves on, and with it, time. Earth evolves, and we follow. There is no escape from change because it's the only permanent thing in this world.

I wish we could never grow up, but that's not what a child would ask for because, at some point, he will need to understand his surroundings while dwelling on the earth. His enjoyment might be shaken; he will start asking questions and then interpreting everything he experiences to understand the reason and purpose of existence in this world:

"Why am I here? Where am I? Who or what am I? Where do I come from? Or 'when' do I come from? Is there a 'where' or 'when' at all? Hey, is there even an 'I'? Do I exist? Am I here? And what's

Endless questions with endless hidden answers. Maybe some answers are in front of us, but we can't see them, for they may have taken the form of signs, while the rest might remain unknown until a specific time or after our death. Should the latter be called otherwise?

"Hey you, wake up! Were you asleep? Or are you like that all the time?"

"Pay attention! Your grades are not so satisfying, so focus on the lesson; otherwise, you won't be happy."

"Sure, sorry, miss, I'm still tired from the nights I spent studying for my chemistry exam."

"Oh yes, the one on which you scored four out of twenty, right?"

"Yes, unfortunately, I didn't understand why—"

"Of course, you didn't because you're so careless. If you stay like that, you'll never succeed in the final exams."

If only people knew what's constantly on your mind. Then, they might pardon you for straying for a moment and forgetting where and when you are in the 'now.' If only your teacher knew what's making you so lost or in another dimension. But does it matter? She only talks about exams and grades. Intelligence is just a matter of memorizing and 'vomiting' what was memorized without questioning the source and goal of what we are learning. Whether you like it or not, it doesn't matter; the initial intention is to adhere to the absolute law to have a so-called 'future.'

Nowadays, people call you crazy for thinking out of the box. If you dare to question things, you'll end up with a bunch of critics and accusations for doubting the undebatable and trying to obtain appropriate answers from inappropriate questions. That judging, unfortunately, spawns from unconsciously chained souls and minds. But being the silent, respectable, lone-wolf guy hides you from the truth and makes the take-in of critics much harder. Stupid people criticize and fill you with sarcasm until you doubt yourself and start feeling worthless or that you're not enough for society.

So, with 'anxiety' as my regular companion, silence ruled me. Although I studied hard, I failed all my chemistry exams. But I never actually liked chemistry or many other subjects, or more specifically, the taught versions of them. Final exams came, and everyone applied. But by some chance, the country went into chaos following economic strikes, and exams weren't corrected. Everyone got a free ticket from high school to the next stage.

"Did you hear what I said?"

"Oh, sorry, I strayed in the sea. No, I wouldn't say I like today's Architecture. It needs to be changed. I can't keep quiet about it; it's been years. Why is architecture so fixed and finished when our lives change and are unfinished? Why should we live in dead cages that don't change nor evolve with us? These cages... they're neither humane nor alive..."

"Okay, so what is your thesis going to be about? I need a summary that respects the given outline and clarifies the idea in the simplest way possible so the audience can easily absorb it. Remember that well, for it's essential to consider for the grading criteria."

"Oh, uhm, well, it is about searching for a true and real architecture that is alive. But the thing is that this matter goes way beyond architecture as a field. It's about how and what it is to exist in the universe to understand the role of architecture and how it should be blended with this cosmos."

"Great! Then, get to work; time is ticking. You don't have much of it, so don't wander away. Don't forget that you must possess something material to present eventually. Good luck; please let me know if you have any questions or concerns."

“Uhm, sure, thank you for everything. I think all is clear.”

Chained Existence

'Grade,' 'Material,' 'Outline,' 'System,' 'Time' ... Where did these terms come from? It's unclear what he meant. Why is everyone always in a hurry? He only cared about a product and buried the rest of what was mentioned as if it was some fantasy. He might not have heard it even. The only thing that mattered to him was obtaining a project that could be listed in the university's files on a specific date and then making it official for the university to demonstrate that it possesses the required competency in front of the authoritative organizations. In that way, they'll guarantee a better reputation and attract more donors and students to join, consequently increasing profits, while my thesis will end up in some drawer. Indeed, quality matters, but it comes second. The gold medal goes to 'profit.' Well, that's not a choice for today's organizations anymore because it is what the whole matrix claims to be a 'necessity to survive.'

After, students take what they learned and set out to start working at different institutions that follow the same modality of the previous ones, where their main target is wealth. The result is a commercial institution whose stage name is 'life,' and a slogan quoting: "where ideas are buried and materialism is revived." The primary interest is to transform us into machines that can follow this materialistic age's fake laws and systems that worship money and recite its rituals every day. It makes us bricks in a wall of retained freedom, vessels of chained existence.

Why have we become so materialistic? What is it with the word 'money' that makes people forget who they are? Is it because the Industrial Age glorified interest and vilified love? When many people became selfish and isolated, architecture their cage of selfishness...

"I see all this potential, and I see it squandered. God damn it, an entire generation pumping gas, waiting tables - slaves with white collars. Advertising has us chasing cars and clothes, working jobs we hate so we can buy shit we don't need. We're the middle children of history, man. No purpose or place. We have no Great War. No Great Depression. Our great war is a spiritual war... Our great depression is our lives. We've all been raised on television to believe that one day we'd all be millionaires, movie gods, and rock stars, but we won't. We're slowly learning that fact. And we're very, very pissed off." —Fight Club, 1999.

Many individuals are so in a hurry to graduate, apply for a job with an excellent salary, purchase a bigger house, a faster car, or a newer cell phone, get married, have kids, and then spend their lives either paying off their debts or stuck in the addiction of chasing a bigger house, a better car, the latest phone, and making more money from work. Their lives will be wasted in becoming more affluent and guiding their kids down the same path. The outcome is a materialistic generation whose only interests are filling their pockets and a better social figure, where the latter is ironically visualized from a distorted perspective.

Why should we spend all our money or be in debt for a more significant, expensive residence, knowing that our current one comfortably accommodates us? And even if it's somehow better, why is it so expensive to settle down, remembering that the earth's lands were initially free of charge? Why should we buy a faster car if the one we own transports us to wherever we want? Or, realizing that transportation shouldn't cost anything because our feet don't require funding to run, why should cars? Cars need gas to run, not money. Why buy the latest phone if the older one performs perfectly? Is it a need or an addiction? What caused this addiction? Why was it caused? And how to cure it?

"No one owns the water.
No one owns the land.
No one owns the oceans.
No one owns the sand.
These are given by our mother; the planet provides for free.
Only by the hands of the greedy, does the earth require a fee." —
Poet Christopher

I believe that the system is corrupt on purpose. We are being remodeled to disciplined automation under the title of safety and security, but never freedom, with salaries added to the equation to cut off our wings by bribing us to forget our real dreams. Wings that could've made anything attainable and taken us wherever we desire. But with the interference of corruption in the matrix, our dreams became the essential elements and necessities of surviving, while everything additional became excessive or magical.

We shouldn't worry about nor pursue such matters, for they are any human being's birthright. We don't have to waste our lives and energy to survive with the minimum and achieve our dreams only when we save some money, when we're old, or when it's too late. But unfortunately, this is the current situation; we either go with the stream or dare to break out of it.

"We used to look up at the sky and wonder at our place in the stars; now we just look down and worry about our place in the dirt"
—Interstellar, 2014.

We are born free. How can we tolerate something chaining us and directing our lives? Doesn't it bother you to see freeborn souls dying from hunger and illness or living in the streets because of their 'poverty'? Why should money be the sole ranking criteria of fascinating beings whom, if you wander into, you'll be lost in immense gardens of ideas and emotions that have the ability and readiness to help, create, innovate, make a huge difference, and show us what real wealth is?

It's because most associate the work-eat-entertainment-sleep cycle with life and consider everything out of the cycle as extra. Few still care about where we came from, why we are here, and where we are going. What are we doing here? Why were we created? What created us? What can we do? What should we do? What matters in this life? Who defines what matters? Will we live after we die? Is death the end? Or is there an afterlife? Will we take anything with us after our death? What should we bring to the hereafter, if there is one out there?

"It's obvious! We're here to pray to God. That's more than enough; nothing else matters. Just work to survive and stop tiring your poor mind. Save it for work; you'll need it. Or use it to weigh up your pockets instead of this weird philosophy of yours."

"That's it? Just for that? Really? Nothing else matters? Are you serious or just disregarding life? So, with all the depth and complexity of this world, you still tell me that we were born for only one purpose: to pray? Rethink it, for what this universe hides is much more than that. The reality that we know could be a dream, and death our dawn, the revealer of all secrets."

"What secrets are there to reveal? God himself said that we are here to pray. Who are you to negate that? You're just an infidel."

Echo in Eternity

The known universe's stars outnumber grains of sand on the Earth's beaches, and the water molecules in one cubic inch of water outnumber the known universe's stars. Yet many individuals only care about surviving and praying. All this universe and its hundred billion galaxies were created for nothing for some; it's just wasted space.

It's not enough to stay alive; We need to be alive. We can live without being alive, and we can die without being dead.

If we keep dwelling on Earth passively, our lives will be squandered or incomplete, for we won't have experienced life fully. It would be like riding a bus in a stunning environment while keeping the curtains closed. But if we dwell on Earth actively, our lives will be meaningful because we will live the utmost adventure. And when death knocks, we will gladly welcome it because we'll know that we'll forever live in the memory of others and only die when the last heart that remembers us stops beating.

No, this doesn't mean we must achieve glory or reach fame. It could simply be planting an idea in the soil of the unquestionable or spending our lives seeking the truth and believing that:

"Everything we carry out in life not only etches in memory but also echoes in eternity."

It's to understand the real value and then thrive in appreciating it.

"So many people live within unhappy circumstances and yet will not take the initiative to change their situation because they are conditioned to a life of security, conformity, and conservatism, all of which may appear to give one peace of mind, but in reality, nothing is more damaging to the adventurous spirit within a man than a secure future. The very basic core of a man's living spirit is his passion for adventure. The joy of life comes from our encounters with new experiences, and hence, there is no greater joy than to have an endlessly changing horizon, for each day to have a new and different sun." —Christopher McCandless.

That is a man who dared. To those who don't know him, *Christopher* was a man who never settled for the lie that we live in today. He believed that the so-called 'society' was deeply corrupt, so he broke out of it and carved his way into the wilderness, believing that the truth was there, that happiness was there. He valued truth above all and sacrificed everything to find it. But he was alone and couldn't endure it for a long time besides his conclusion that happiness is only real when shared. He eventually perished after he sadly starved to death, leaving behind a legend that to this day is spoken of. You cannot but keep wondering about his eagerness to leave 'civilization' behind and walk into the wild...

Could nature be a part of the answer? Could sunrays be a signal for something? Could the wind be directing us somewhere? Could the stars be a map for someone? Could we be unconsciously working with nature? Could we be an intrinsic part of a massive divine plan? Everything is possible, yet impossible. How can we be certain of anything when 'certitude' is not certain?

Well, we have something to start with: thoughts. Our brains weren't created by coincidence, and the unknown purposely remained mysterious so that we could experience something marvelous while riding life's ocean of time: the sensitivity of being alive.

Imagine a world where everything is known and fixed in advance. What we'll turn into in the future, what we will look like, how often we'll fall in love, whom we'll marry, how we'll meet each other, how many children we'll have, when we'll die, how we'll die, who will die first, etc.... If you recognize all that from the beginning, life loses its taste. Its predictability and 'finished' version would forever restrain you from feeling zeal and passion.

You won't persevere in anything anymore if you perceive at birth that you won't bear children, will pick up a lethal disease, or perish at an early age. Even if positive things were known, such as that you'll attain greatness or gain wealth and fame in the future, you would've lost the energy of putting effort into it and preferred waiting till it takes effect. And that's only accurate if we are not the ones who determine such matters, which is an entirely different theme yet to be discussed.

I've always appreciated the notion of being lost in the unknown. Ironically, the mystery is both scary and beautiful simultaneously. Experiencing life's unknowns and deep secrets is somehow enjoyable, no matter how hard it gets.

What's the essence of life if everything is known, and what's the purpose of existence if life is already clear, finished, or, in other words, dead?

"To live" differs from "to be alive." It's in the process of living and discovering that we embrace life, experience life in every breath and heartbeat, learn and wonder about things, and seek more to be interpreters instead of spectators. That is what keeps us active in life, in other words, alive.

10:00 a.m. — Incoming call:

"Hey, how are you? I'm considering having lunch at that fancy restaurant I once mentioned. It's two hours from here, near that weird forest. Are you in?"

"Oh, hey, uhm, well, of course, just give me some time to get back to you, for I might be a little busy today. I'll let you know in an hour."

"Okay, fine, I'll be waiting for your call..."

1:45 p.m. — Voice message:

"Hey, it's about time. Why aren't you answering my calls? Are you dead?"

Broken Bondage

Why only restaurants? Isn't there anything else to do? Why should we constrain ourselves to the same activity? It's like a two-hour trip to the kitchen. That forest he mentioned seems a better option, for it allows some adventure and is a new experience. The problem is that he can't be told this, for he won't understand. He'll eventually assume I'm making excuses because I don't enjoy his company. It's best to make it seem like I didn't hear my phone and forgot about the whole thing...

If only we could go somewhere else to discover a new region or culture instead... It will be much more suspenseful than sitting around a table and babbling about work, people, mundane activities, and wishes. We crave to open our hearts occasionally while comfortably having a delicious meal, but it doesn't need to be done in a café or restaurant every time. Do we even think about that? Hey, perhaps that's the whole issue...

"Morpheus: The Matrix is everywhere. It is all around us. Even now, in this very room. You can see it when you look out your window or when you turn on your television. You can feel it when you go to work... when you go to church... when you pay your taxes. It is the world that has been pulled over your eyes to blind you from the truth.

Neo: "What truth?"

Morpheus: "That you are a slave, Neo. Like everyone else, you were born into bondage. Into a prison that you cannot taste or see or touch. A prison for your mind."'

—*The Matrix, 1999.*

We were born and thrown into this corrupt matrix that glorifies routine and conventionality. 'Normal' individuals — let's call them that for now— survive daily, then spend their free time in places of distraction that don't require thinking or effort, like restaurants, pubs, cinemas, etc. These are the available options for individuals who work or study like slaves for more hours than a human body and soul should endure per day. They won't have the energy to do anything more than entertainment because they are exhausted from their jobs and the worries that come with them. That's what they will think about or would prefer to do.

Our minds parallel our environment, and the latter is crooked. Our free time is not free at all; It's designed to function in one way, so why bother considering various options? We are unconsciously captured in a very spacious virtual prison whose bars are cleverly hidden. Its main rule is simple: Kneel, and we'll keep you safe and secure!

But there's something that, if fearlessly followed, will always be a glitch in the matrix; the heart.

The heart knows what it needs, but the challenge is to wake the mind from illusion. To accomplish that, we must break free from or cure the matrix so that the mind can function freely and correctly.

9:00 p.m. — Voice message: "Dumbass."

He's right, but the matrix must be blamed, not me. And it simply doesn't end here...

At the dawn of the Industrial Revolution, a significant modification in our behavior was implemented. The rise and domination of the machine altered many things, most importantly, the humane value of things. We saw the surge of materialism when interest and profit became the primary rate of things, whereas other humane factors became an option.

Moreover, this shift led to money becoming a more vigorous ruler over all else, and everything was designed accordingly.

Thus, people's mentality shifted from humane to economic when the system's demand for money increased. That was resolved by them working longer hours, which resulted in less social interaction and boredom.

Subsequently, ways of communication were created to work with this transition, such as social media on all its platforms. We started talking to and interacting with screens instead of humans because we no longer wanted or had no time to meet people face to face except for a few robbed hours, like in restaurants. This separation from one another weakened genuine connection and love while bolstering judgment, jealousy, and envy because a very critical area was exploited from all of what was just mentioned: Narcissism.

Social media exposes our intimate and private lives, which nobody must or should be aware of. Wherever we are, whomever we're with, whatever we do, whenever we do it, we post for the public's approval, for arrogance, or out of boredom and the need to connect with people, which the matrix deepened all by its exhausting mechanisms that hijacked most of our time. Still, we justify that under the title of love. Consciously or unconsciously, it doesn't matter; we're all in the same pit. Few still do it for knowledge, for love, whereas the majority lost the zeal to do it for themselves, for passion, and instead accepted to live in the most dangerous prison in the present day: The jail of mundanity and of what other people think.

Moreover, along with money, television, and other things, these 'distractions' create artificial comfort for us, so we think these are the finest things anyone could dream of acquiring. Even love was substituted by pornography, and many blindly welcomed the concept after it was filmed in a way that made it seem like true love. They enjoyed discussing it along with watching intimate and filthy actions as if they were very ordinary while missing the ugly, disgusting truth of rape and exploitation. That ended wistfully, with many deciding to abandon love and pursue pleasure. But if stuff like social media and pornography are free, then we are the products.

"If you're not paying for the product, then you are the product" —The Social Dilemma, 2020.

Why? They make us live in a virtual world where we think we own everything while we don't own anything. We're not the problem; we're never the problem:

Nonetheless, as the famous quote says, *"Comfort is the biggest drug: give an individual good food, cheap entertainment, and infinite sex, then watch how he throws his ambitions away and how the world changes him. Deprive him of these three, and watch how he changes the world. The comfort zone is where dreams die."*

But in our case, it's not the world that changes them because the world at its origin is pure; it's the matrix. We must seek discomfort, and what do we tell it when it comes?

"We want more, and hell can be a home, for comfort is a drug and won't make us grow."

"I wanted movement and not a calm course of existence. I wanted excitement and the chance to sacrifice myself for my love. I felt in myself a superabundance of energy which found no outlet in our quiet life" —Leo Tolstoy.

Unchained Zeal

Fauna gives no damn about money!
Seen any mourn a falling currency?!
Noticed? They eat, play, and travel freely!

Mundanity limits, passive acquiescence encages, comfort deceives, bondage enslaves, and a calm course of existence kills. How can you live passively? Don't you like intensity? To keep evolving infinitely?

"You're faking it! If you love me, you'll sacrifice some of your dreams because I have my own, too. You cannot fly high if you truly care for me, but it seems you don't."

"Yes, I do, you should be assured of that... I'll make sure to fulfill your dreams, but I also can't deny mine; understand that..."

The Universe Loves

At times, you come across a type of love that is both deep and rootless. Beautiful yet unpredictable, you may not take much time to fall in love with each other, even if you're not sure about it. Perhaps something in them is unique; you don't know what to call it. Your souls may have met before, in another time or universe. But even though the affection is profound, they will not always appreciate how much you love. They might even assume that your dreams take priority over them; thus, they try to shrink your ambitions.

That kind of love is strange; you simultaneously experience extreme happiness and doubt. You feel that you must provide it with everything you're capable of to make it work, and your most profound emotions, considered hard to divulge, are quickly revealed. Everything humane you suppressed, for whatever reason, will beautifully display itself without your permission.

You think that you'll be able to control it, but the truth is that it alone will control you because it doesn't limit itself nor remains behind the danger line of logic and reason, especially if it's generated from the depths of the soul. If it's a powerful one, you're in another dimension with different laws of logic and physics. And that's the artistry of it... It's the most potent remedy for happiness you'll ever receive because you'll obliterate all the pain and suffering of the past. You'll be so attached to it because you assume you'll lose everything if it's lost.

"Drop the idea that attachment and love are one thing. They are enemies. It is 'attachment' that destroys all love." —Osho.

Nevertheless, things are confusing now... your love becomes tired and suspicious: Why sacrifice dreams for love? That doesn't make sense at all. Shouldn't both be the same thing? A flower is loved by being watered, not plucked. Love isn't to control but rather to grow. Is this even real love? Perhaps they needed to 'be loved' instead of love, which is a different matter. So, after unleashing your inner lover, it froze in a strange dilemma of a simple yet convoluted crossroads of dreams and love. Thus, for it to take the right turn, it necessitated comprehending real love.

So, what is love? Many people state that with it, we shift to the most beautiful version of ourselves. Some claim that without it, our 'logical' side ameliorates and gives our ambitions a better chance of being achievable. Others argue that it has gone astray and needs to be found so that we can work properly. Perspectives differ, but the image is transparent to those who genuinely desire to 'see.'

"The universe pretends to be made of matter. Secretly, it is made of love." —*Rumi.*

It astonishingly performs that from its vastest to tiniest creation... Look around you; contemplate how the universe loves: watch how the sun wakes up to warm the earth so it doesn't freeze. Study how the ground stores the sun's heat to use at night, for the same purpose, when the yellow planet sleeps. Examine how the atmosphere incubates us to protect us from attacking meteors. Stray how the moon and stars lighten the earth at its darkest times. Read how forming and exploding stars paint the night sky with stunning artistic compositions. Notice how mountains dig three times their observed height to hold the ground and prevent it from shaking. Consider how the rain fills the thirst of earth's green beings. Study how the sea sacrifices to receive all the salt cleaned by the rain to purify the world. Understand how the air modifies itself to maintain our needed percentage of oxygen and aerifies our bodies.

Notice how nature paints the globe with its palette. Read how trees purify the air and feed beings in need. Watch how snow covers our mother with a stunning white dress. See how the sky makes us feel at peace with its relaxing mood. Observe how clouds entertain us through magnificent theatrical sceneries throughout the day.

Look how animals, no matter how dangerous they are, give everything to bring food back to their children and enjoy their company. Notice how even a lion can be tamed if loved and treated right. Study how even a snake's poison can be used to produce medicaments. Consider how wolves defend their pack to the last breath. See how pets can compensate for children. Listen to how birds compose love songs and teach dance lessons. Gaze at how butterflies sparkle in their flaunting beauty. Read how bees unite flowers in love with each other by spreading their pollens in exchange for being fed. Examine how flies, although annoying, eat and clean our detritus. Watch how ants work as a disciplined team to survive the harshest days.

Of course, focus on how we are an intrinsic part of that circle. We, if full of love, can help an elderly, heal a diseased, cure a psycho, breed a child, educate the ignorant, guide the sightless, carry the disabled, tame the monsters, grow seeds, decorate cities, glorify unity, fight for freedom, sacrifice for duty, die for honor, bloom the earth, spread cultures, embrace religions, accept differences, and most importantly, kill fanaticism.

"Your mother made that happen. She's the one to blame for everything. Accept the consequences with your siblings."

"Hey! Don't talk about her like that or accept yourselves that it'll be the end of a once-upon-a-time loving relationship! I know what I saw, and you won't have the legitimacy of oppressing her..."

"How dare you talk to us like that! You're disrespectful and inequitable."

Life's Theatre

But sometimes, love fails when it faces a stronger opponent: Truth. Love might sometimes be the death of truth because of its tremendous and unexplainable ability to make you cast aside reason. But sometimes, when reason is mature in the form of truth, and the consequences of your choice will go awry if you choose wrong, truth is the death of love. Times when you are put in the middle of a rope-pulling game where right and wrong are the opposing players, and you don't realize which side you must pull. Or, you try to find a way out of the game in the hope of saving both truth and love.

Well, that might be possible because the paradox is that frequently, both parties consider themselves fighting for the truth. The truth is that both are conceptually right because each sees it from their perspective. How? It's because that exact viewpoint is not always molded with logic. It is usually built from personal experiences and anonymous feelings, which were sculpted through time and kept concealed from the public eye.

How? We've all been actors on joyful and sorrowful stages in life's theatre, haven't we?

What we encounter while breathing is sometimes hard for the human heart to carry. Love, hatred, pleasure, pain, life, death, success, failure, admiration, jealousy, pride, shame, honor, disgrace, etc.... Unfortunately, our hearts weren't cast from steel; they're tiny, fragile entities that cannot endure much and could easily break if hurt too much.

Furthermore, the heart is somehow connected to its upstairs neighbor. The latter doesn't understand emotions but gets affected by them. Its way of thinking, varying from one individual to another, shifts from running on logic to emotion when its downstairs friend gets twinged more than its maximum endurance. It could even reach a point when it empties its vessel, burns it, and then rents a room from its downstairs neighbor's apartment forever if the hurting reaches its peak to compensate for its low production.

While settling there, it comes up with new regulations and laws for visitors stating: 'Individuals seeking logic are not allowed in under any circumstances for I can no longer comprehend, nor am I willing to do so. Only sentiments are welcome inside, primarily from those I adore, for they are above everyone. And please, do not bother me if it's avoidable. Finally, remember to always knock on the door softly and slowly whenever you need something, or it won't open. Thank you.'

Some traits, buried deep down, can't be changed. People are who they are because of what they have been through. And we cannot heal everyone from pain because some can't even tolerate the idea of overcoming it anymore.

So, after comprehending how humans get disturbed and unintentionally lose parts of themselves, how can you play the challenge game knowing that the players are unconsciously on the same side? If a team loses or wins, will it be temporarily delusional only to conclude after a while that the game has never been and will never be fair? There will be neither losers nor winners, just more conflicts and misunderstandings caused by hidden undiscovered patterns, which none of the players realize or admit...

The answer is kindness. To gently play with everyone or not to play at all. This way, nobody gets hurt by you or accuses you of being mean and unfair. It's the only way everyone wins, the only way love wins. This is, of course, if one of the parties is unconscious, which usually is the case in this insane world where only the insane are sane because they know too much yet never know too much enough.

—November 17, 2020—

"We are the manipulators of the country, and we do whatever we desire. You, people, are just here to applaud us for whatever we offer. Let the man or woman among you dare to rebel, and you'll see how we'll make you suffer in ways you have never heard of..."

(Yelling) "Die you, filthy creatures!"

Death of Love

But what if the other party is conscious? What if it's dirty and uses fake love as soap to clean itself and hide the slipping dirt from the public eye? What should we do then when we realize the dirty truth and know that love doesn't work here because the dirt's too thick to be removed by real love? At that point, the public climbs onto the roof of silence and declares that now's the time: Now love dies. Today begins melting feelings to harden monsters who can't be tamed because they've been silent for so long. They've reached a point where they become heartless and will devour whoever tries to persecute them or rub their scars.

Many are aware of the beauty of the universe they dwell in but deliberately decide to neglect it for some reason, cited by an evil-spirited creature that doesn't include the word 'Love' in its dictionary: Satan. With his shows, he deceives weak and greedy people to make them slip into a world where the light vanished a long time ago. But Satan brightens everything dark; He tries to convince us to live an easy life where everything's permissible. But even if the world's changing, we mustn't change with it. What he offers them is something great yet dangerous: Authority.

Authority is a double-edged sword; a shapeshifter that can shift to its worst shape if greedy individuals reach it before the ascetics. They can change the flag's ownership and emblem to something they claim is for the betterment of the country. But this is not the truth; it is just a delusion. They only pursue their personal goals without caring for the citizens' interests and healthy lives. And that decisively makes the latter bury love and resurrect ruthlessness to maintain their rights and reclaim their homeland.

— August 4, 2020 — *Boom! (Blood, Screams) *

"Seriously? Are you threatening your people? The ones who got you all to the point where you're now, and who, without their blessings, this would've never occurred? But you and your foreign partners in crime deceived them and made it look different. Look at what you've done! The country's suffering because of your greed; hundreds of wounded and dead… we'll never forget August 4th. Blood will make the revolution stronger than ever; we won't be afraid but rather be more eager to bring you down. Don't think that your death is your escape and end; It is the beginning of your punishment. And because we 'love' you so much, we'll offer you your punishment before you even die."

"They may take our lives, but they'll never take our freedom."
—Braveheart, 1995.

On Lebanon

You've had enough of this war,
You're the darkness of a star…
You're not dead but full of dust;
You're what needs to be a must!
We'll get you back to the clouds!
Where you're more than ever loud!
We'll force you to peace, be bound!
We'll beat them and make you proud.

"Hey! Don't go that far; God will punish them in life or the hereafter; they won't escape trial."

"God? How does he punish them if we don't revolt? Aren't we the ones who decide their fate?"

"No, dear, such things are beyond humans' free will and are controlled by a much higher power."

Let tyrants feel satisfied!
In life, thinking they could hide
When summoned after they die
And punished for whoever cried,
By a fire that never runs out of supplies,
To keep forever burning them alive.
That day will come by order of the sky!

Fated Freedom

Do we determine what arises? Or is it determined before it arises? Do we need what has arisen? Or can we raise what we need? Do we need it for our growth? Or can we grow without its need? Do we know what we need for our growth? Or does our growth know what we need? Could what we need arise in another scenario for our growth? Or has it arisen in one only scenario, for it knows what we need to grow? Are we free? Or does fate rule our lives? And what defines freedom and fate?

"I don't believe in the gods' existence. Man is the master of his own fate, not the gods. The gods are man's creation to give answers that they are too afraid to give themselves." —Vikings, 2013-2020.

Perhaps we are not fated. Fate might not be fixed but may be a changing element that parallels our will. Maybe the world opens and closes the doors we alone decide to knock on. Perhaps fate isn't magic, but instead, we are. We are the ones who build and demolish doors. We make everything we desire work according to the energy we put into the universe: Our past, present, future, economy, politics, friends, enemies, homes, health, jobs, love, children, etc.... Even birth and death are sanctioned by our actions.

A newborn child? Yes, we decided to have children. Dead? Yes, they weren't careful or didn't sustain their life well during existence's journey. A revolution? We rebelled and punished corrupt politicians to change the country's situation. Without us, none of that would've materialized. Our free will is free; we alone govern its freedom, and fate is but an excuse for the weak and the fearful ones who find it very difficult to dare to act. Some are genuinely convinced that their fate was determined before they were born, while others pretend to be convinced as an excuse to sit back and do nothing to alter their condition.

—August 23, 2013—

*Boom! (Screams) *

That day is still remembered when the 'Al-Salam' mosque was bombed while full of people who came to pray. When I arrived for prayers on time, I wanted to sit outside near the main door as usual, but I couldn't find a place. So, I had to move to the main hall instead. When the sermon was about to end, a bomb detonated. Almost everyone sitting outside died. If I hadn't been inside, I probably wouldn't have been able to write this now.

And that's not all: the criminal who blew up the mosque wanted it right after the prayer when people go out and return home. But the sheik's sermon was unexpectedly longer that day. Therefore, the blast occurred when a large group of people was still inside, which saved them.

Hence, both facts that there was no place to sit outside and the sheik's surprisingly long sermon make you wonder if you are free in everything and whether both are coincidences. But you cannot help but think that something didn't want you to die that day; maybe your time hasn't come yet. Perhaps you cannot decide when or how to die. Well, maybe you can't even choose to be born. True, your parents decided to have a child, but you didn't choose to exist. Someone else could've been born back then, or couldn't they? Maybe it wasn't your parents' decision after all. This alone changes the previous notion that we are entirely free.

Some may declare that if the criminal hadn't made a mistake, or if it had been another criminal's operation, everyone would have perished. But no, an uncontrolled error isn't a choice; It's more than that: it's a miracle.

A blind person whose sight is naturally restored is a miracle. A disabled individual who walks again is a miracle. A man diagnosed with cancer who lives after being told that he'll die on a specific date is a miracle. A woman who suffers from poverty because of her oppressing husband, who unexpectedly dies and leaves her a fortune, is a miracle. A girl rejected by a university just to be suddenly admitted into a far better one is a miracle. A child who has evolved into a great leader after learning from his painful past is a miracle. A soul who was obligated to leave their neighborhood for another one where they met their soulmate is a miracle.

"What is meant for you will reach you even if it is beneath two mountains, and what isn't meant for you won't reach you even if it is between your two lips." —Ali Ben Abi Talib.

Hence, you start to wonder how fate works, knowing we are free to choose everything. But then you look at some miracles and how things turn and change, and then you deduct that fate is a door: sometimes it opens by itself, and sometimes it opens when you decide to knock. However, in either case, it doesn't mean you're fated to enter. You are still free to knock on other doors. But then a ghost intervenes without your permission; It's called experience. It carries your past, dreams, and psychological logic formed from the lessons of sorrow you never chose. And without thinking, you realize which door to choose. Then you wonder again if the whole issue is fate or freedom.

That's the paradox... We are free to determine our wishes, but our wishes are determined for us. They are controlled by the deepest desires that we are born with and that we'll forever pursue.

We think we are free, but our freedom is fated, and therefore our fate is free.

So, are they two components, or do they function as one? And can we change things, or were the things we change never meant to remain the same? Could there be another world in which our lives are different, or are they the same in every known reality if any other exists?

"Did I mention to you that yesterday's dream came true today? Oh my God, it was like a sign or something..."

"This is shocking... hey... how? What happened in your dream? But... Well, could... other worlds exist?"

Dreamy Reality

Glimpses, Glimpses of desires, Desires of a heart, Heart of a lover, Lover of dreams, Dreams of love, Love of truth, Truth of existence, Existence of life, Life of a passenger, Passenger of time, Time of living, living life, Life in existing, existing truly, True love, loving dreams, Dreaming of love, Love of a heart, Heart of desires, Desires of glimpses… it's all for nothing without glimpses.

It is claimed that dreams are reflections of our desires blended with our past; everything we wish is a deep need for a desire born from our past and the experiences we've had, which have influenced how we perceive life and defined our wants. Well, that might be possible if everything we are is molded by this universe's laws of existence, like life's known sciences.

However, having learned that there might be a possibility of existence in different universes, the previous theory might have been misinterpreted. Perhaps dreams are more than a result of equations and emotions; they could be glimpses from the future that will be real one day, regardless of how we act till then. Or even a real-life somewhere unknown, unexplored, into where our earthly roots extend. That is indeed viable when presuming that we are rooted here. But what if we aren't? What if the reality we experience is not lonely?

"Dreams feel real while we're in them. It's only when we wake up that we realize something was actually strange." —Inception, 2010.

Some allege that there are copies of you in different universes, and each copy believes that their world is real, while other worlds are just imaginations. So,

Can your reality be the imagination of your copy and your imagination a reality of your copy? Do our imaginations also have copies that each one thinks its world is virtual? Or is what we imagine real in another universe, and our reality is the imagination of one of our copies?

That is to say, the glimpses we see genuinely occur in other worlds... According to quantum physics, every time you have two options and choose one, the universe splits into two, where you choose the other option in another universe...

That blurs the boundary between reality and dream. We are no longer sure if we are real. Perhaps this line separating us from the truth becomes blurred when we tolerate the idea of other copies and worlds, where our realities and imaginations don't resemble even the ones we are consciously living.

Maybe this world is not an introvert; it is credible that it is an extrovert collaborating with other worlds following an ambiguous strategy—one we humans don't know how to read yet. Everything is probable yet improbable.

What if all that crops up here crops up there in a different scenario? What if our lives took different paths elsewhere? What if the people we meet here are not included in our lives out there? What if the sorrows and joys which take effect on the earth are different in another reality? What if fate and freedom get diverse definitions in various realities? Or even get implemented in ways distinct from this known world?

Perhaps what materializes in our world needs to materialize for other worlds to have unique scenarios, and all scenarios somehow reflect on our scenario and make it viable, and vice versa. Our life itself could be the water; the more we work for it, the more the unknown world grows. It is imaginable that if what we desire doesn't take place here, it'll do there. So, this adds a lot to the entire theory of existence and its laws or maybe questions it.

Did you know that only 1% of the visible light spectrum is visible to humans? 99% of the world we live in is invisible to us! Most of our existence is obscured, so how can we ever settle for what we can see and neglect the idea that something is present beyond our slight vision?

"There are known knowns. These are things we know that we know. There are known unknowns. That is to say, there are things that we know we don't know. But there are also unknown unknowns. There are things we don't know we don't know." — Donald Rumsfeld.

The universe is infinite, and with it are possibilities. Different realities and dreams can exist out there, living their lives and fantasizing about their imaginations. We may not even be real or may not have dreams. The vastness and ambiguousness of the cosmos make you wander beyond anything.

Perhaps we, our copies, realities, and dreams, are just one entity dispersed across billions of planets. Maybe they are all just thoughts, and the immensity of the universe is not what we picture: Couldn't we be a brain cell in a larger being? All we had been, are, and will be are only thoughts of one more extraordinary being who created us, our knowns and unknowns. They direct all known and unknown universes with a tight and coherent plan: A mind-blown truth lurking somewhere, somehow...

"Have you heard of the latest casualty report? It is reported that the number of deaths and injuries is increasing dramatically. God help us; this virus is not easy to handle. Save yourself and get vaccinated."

"Oh, that's heart-breaking. May they all rest in peace... Well, I'll think about that."

Needle of Light

It's a mysterious plan. What needs to change? What should we learn from this? Why all this chaos? The world is changing, and people are suffering—we can see that—millions of dead, wounded, hardships, and misery. Fear is roaming the planet freely. Everybody is hiding, sheltering, and praying. But somehow, even with all the layers of darkness being woven into our skins, there's still a feeling that the needle is made of light.

Sometimes, I wonder what would be the words of nature's broken silence... Of all the scars it gets from humans' mistreatment that is leading to its paleness and death. Without uttering a single word, it endures everything that hurts it and asks for nothing more than peace and love. It fades from pain and grows with love. Only those willing to love it will be able to grow it and grow with it. All of this was known from its silence. I wonder how much pain and love are hidden behind silence.

Perhaps the virus is not random; Watch closer: people are cleaner, family ties are more robust, filthy places are empty, and most importantly, the earth is healing. As you can see, if we look at what's going on from a brighter side, we'll notice its covered beauty.

Yes, on the one hand, people are dying. Maybe it's time for them to go, and we might be next, and that's fine. But the stuff emerging, on the other hand, is undoubtedly enhancing the universe. Mother Earth is reclaiming its power and spreading her children throughout its kingdom again to take back control from its enemy: artificiality.

After all, it doesn't matter; it was and will always be the most remarkable delusion. We think we own life when we have it, but even so, look at us now... we're wondering what to do with it. The truth is that nothing needs it to work, especially not us. Food is grown and needs water, and water is everywhere. Clothes need materials, and the sources of the latter are everywhere. Electricity demands energy, and energy comes from the sun or fuels underground. And shelters require nothing more than construction and effort... Money confines us in a cage that doesn't exist. You'd say that the more we have, the happier we are. I'll tell you that you're right because it can enlarge the cage. But the truth is that the cage's door is always open, but we are so stuck inside the matrix that it has made us crippled, and we got used to it because we don't see any other way. We're so dependent on the matrix that we will challenge the impossible to protect it because if it collapses, we'll collapse. Yes, it's unfortunate, but it's not too late to break free from what they have taught us: To unlearn what we learned.

And with this pandemic, the truth has prevailed: money's nothing compared to health. It's nothing more than custom paper and cannot be used when it matters. What followed was that those big and wealthy companies and institutions closed their doors when fear came knocking. None of what they used to provide for the public under the title of 'Survival' survived, except the theory itself. Insurances, syndicates, safety, security, etc., all cracked and got exposed for what they are: the truth that we can and should live without them. Yes, we don't need a government to guide us. That's what they've been hiding for so long; we can live on our terms.

Do you know that thousands die each day from hunger and poverty, much more than the deaths caused by COVID-19 (if, of course, the latter's numbers aren't exaggerated)? But this is not mentioned because it's not in the government's interest. Even the vaccine might be made to help implant something inside us to change our bodies so that they could control us from the inside, whereas before, they used to control us from the outside through smartphones and many other tools. Well, a way to alter human RNA was recently invented, so who knows if some decide to use that to weaken our immune system instead of strengthening it? Many who have already been vaccinated have been infected again or died from Covid-19. Anything is possible when the same people who designed this virus also developed a vaccine for it. Some "Follow the Law" individuals will overreact now and call me a fool, unaware that the vaccine could be another invention to spy on and control us more than ever and that the law is the biggest outlaw and thus cannot be trusted.

"A 2005 film titled "V for Vendetta" is about a totalitarian dictatorship that gains its power by creating a society of fear due to an alleged virus spreading throughout the world. In the film, the media pushes fear-based propaganda on the television screen of every household and the city streets. The authoritarian dictator promises security but not freedom. The constant theme of "this is for your safety" is repeated throughout the film. Most importantly, the film ends with society waking up and the corrupt, fascist regime is dismantled. What year is the film set? ... 2020." —Roger Ebert, 2006.

I repeat, the movie's scenes occur in 2020. It's as if someone knew, 15 years ago, what would happen today and wanted to alert us to the filthiness of the current regime. Do you know that *Stanley Kubrick*, the director of a 1999 movie called "Eyes Wide Shut," who tried to expose an evil, sick organization manipulating the world, was killed the same year his film was released? They claim that the cause of death was a heart attack during sleep. Wow, what a coincidence. Perhaps I will also suddenly disappear after publishing this book. Well, you'll be 100% sure I was correct then. Even the famous "*The Simpsons*" series continues to surprise us by revealing many things that happened exactly as the series showed years ago. Is that a coincidence, too?

Furthermore, a conspiracy theorist named David Icke has published over 20 books exposing secret organizations' hidden plans and practices. This resulted in him being banned from Twitter, too.

Don't you wonder why the government always promises us safety and security but never freedom? That's because they don't want us to be free, nor to discover that the cure is within us, that the greatest delusion is the theory that we need a government or have limitations! They want to bury the veracity that nature knows the truth, that the stars know the way, and we must only believe... That we're not alone, and nothing is random. They may be able to cast darkness over the universe's fabric for a while, but nature always knows how to weave that with a needle of light. In the end, nature always wins.

'" I fear neither death nor pain."
"What do you fear, my lady?"
"A cage. To stay behind bars until use and old age accept them and all chance of valor has gone beyond recall or desire."' —Lord of the Rings, 2002.

I fear the fear of death more than death, for death is real, but its fear is not. Death is once, but if I fear, I will die before I die. So, I won't fear what's not real, so that I don't die before I die. And I won't fear what's not real so that I don't 'make' what's not real real.

If you want us to be dead, we'll be glad to die, even if we're not ready. We won't live in fear because we believe whatever happens is based on your wisdom. That's why we're at peace with it, prepared for whatever you put on the table with open arms, a smile, and a steady heart.

Nature is aware of the situation and how to implement its strategy to resolve what some don't desire to fix. Many declare that we're on the verge of collapse or in the most bottomless pit that history has ever seen. But no, they are wrong. The world is more than just ups and downs; everything was wisely planned from the very start. This is not the end of the beginning. But could it be the beginning of the end? The beautiful birth of a new era? Or is it just the return to ourselves, the return to humanity?

Perfect Flaws

'" What do you think happens when we die, Keanu Reeves?"
"I know that the ones who love us will miss us."'
—Keanu Reeves, in an interview with Stephen Colbert.

I was stray in an apartment, one which they left after they died yesterday, and is where we reside today after they worked all their lives to purchase it. Tomorrow, we will die and leave the houses where others will reside after having worked all our lives to buy them. Suddenly, my straying stopped when I heard a cat's meow. She craved the food that I stopped eating while straying. This struck me, and I asked myself: what if the food is my residence, and my straying is my death? Why should I keep it till I die and let the cat grab it afterward when I can continue to provide for it while I live? In the end, all the savings of the people who died were gone, and they took nothing with them. This is because nothing travels with us but our work and experiences. The only things the world will remember us by.

"You act like mortals in all that you fear, and like immortals in all that you desire." —Seneca.

Let me ask you something: What kind of life does a column witnessing the death of many have? Hundreds of layers of paper and other names are yet to come. Why do we act like immortals? Seeking only money, forgetting what we'll become; A memory, a layer of time.

We keep searching for artificial perfection in everything we carry out in life: perfect work and leisure times, perfectly shaped objects, perfect straight spaces or rooms, perfectly distributed room functions, a 'perfect' salon that has never been touched for guests, a perfect rectangular door, a 'perfect' one-meter-high window, perfectly aligned tiles, perfect proportions, perfectly organized cities, etc.... This is reflected in everything, including Architecture. We can see that in the superfluously regulated world. Pre-determined parcels, delineated streets, building blocks, land setbacks, mass, bulkiness, etc.... This led to the standardization and suppression of products where mechanical cleanness and numerical efficiency determined the product's value, while beauty became an option.

Why all this noisy stuff? Why can't we sleep in the kitchen and eat in the bedroom? Why don't we wear the informal clothes we like for formal events? Why should we only eat three times a day? Why must tiles be aligned and modular? And why should cities follow unnecessary restrictions?

Just stare at the poetry of natural elements such as clouds, stars, trees, plants, flowers, grass, etc.... None of them has mechanical perfection. Instead, they are perfectly formed by geometrical flaws and are in continuous change and evolution. Forms that are not limited to well-known geometric systems: they possess variable and multi-layered environments instead of static volumes, such as dynamic and chaotic grids rather than orthogonal ones, and thrive in the art of creating 'Boundlessness,' where the unstable geometry of the contour dissolves the form of the object in the environment. This leads us to 'live our environment' instead of living in our environment.

Life isn't perfect; our bodies aren't perfect, so why should things be perfect? It's our flaws that make us evolve, and it's our imperfections that make us perfect.

"Maybe things should remain somehow unfinished and ambiguous; we must think of them as 'almost things': open-ended, inviting appropriation and misuse, like structures that are necessarily unfinished and are begging for something to happen. A framework for life, or a boundary that's open...." —nArchitects

It's to appreciate things' ephemerality and embrace their free-changing images or notions that continue redefining their perceptions. It is not a matter of unconnected pieces within the whole, but rather the whole, complicated by many connected pieces.

Human life and our bodies are unfinished, like nature. That is why we enjoy nature: because we are both alive.

Therefore, couldn't Architecture also be alive if its boundary dissolves within the world in a way that makes us humans experience its incomplete process of being rather than its complete version, the same way we experience our own lives?

Perhaps making something imperfect or organic is only possible if it is handmade, for it's our humanity that makes it beautifully flawed or, in other words, humane.

In his book 'The Phenomenon of Life,' Christopher Alexander (2002) discusses 'Real beauty' rather than beauty. It is based on what makes us feel, whether a thing is alive, and its degree of life. The author claims that physics and biology define an object's mechanical order or geometry, not the order that touches us. He criticizes objects that are 'Self-producing biological machines' and believes everything must be a single system. Therefore, it's not about the geometry of a thing but the geometry of the entire system to which it belongs. It's to invent 'Non-living matter that completes the living organism,' criticizing anyone who tries to perfect the geometry of an object alone and be convinced that nothing perfect can genuinely be alive because life itself is damaged.

It cannot be perfect in a transient universe. It is proud of being full of flaws that aren't random but relatively well-structured and make life perfect—an absolute perfection. Thus, we must confidently embrace our blemishes, for, after all, we were, are, and will always be humans...

We keep forgetting that we're humans, decaying beings being decayed in a decayed being, the universe itself, designed for a decaying time, timed to decay with time. And what's 'time'? Time is just understanding that we are only one breath away from the afterlife.

Contemplate the stars... What do you see? Yes, you're both something and nothing: An intrinsic factor in shaping this vast universe and a piece of it, yet when you look at the stars, you'll know that you and your problems are infinitesimally small. You think you own a lot in this world but don't even own your atoms; it's only your time to use them. You're a star within a star, some atoms in the universe, yet billions of stars exist. Existence is both something and nothing at once...

However, at the same time, that something you are made of is stunning. How? Well, it is alleged that just before you die, your whole life flashes before your eyes in a show of a few minutes. It doesn't happen chronologically, but according to the most intense emotional moments: strength, love, ache... all. It'll be a movie where your emotions are the actors, with few resonating words that shake them up. And that's not all; you'll also feel what others have felt. What every character you met along the road of your existence sensed from your energy. So be sure that nothing goes away, and everything will make you aware of what you were and what will become of you in the hereafter.

Thus, only your deeds can replace you in people's memories after your time is up. Your body will decompose, and its borrowed atoms will merge with and return to their origin, nature. They will fly and dance everywhere to form new things and creatures, but they will always pretend they died with us.

"You exist in time, but you belong to eternity." —Osho.

Stray in multiple layers of time,
In how things begin, while others end,
Leaving existential traces behind,
Atoms of death, whereon life depends.
I wondered what would become of mine,
Whenever my soul leaves and ascends.
I'm not, but they truly are divine;
Taking new forms, but always pretend…

"So, if all creatures live and die, and then their atoms roam the world and transform into other beings, are we related?"

"Oh yes, we are all children of one mother, and she was said to be so powerful and stunning."

Vessels of Stars

At the dawn of creation, when nothing yet existed, all the energy particles of the universe were compressed into an infinitely dense and hot tiny point. This super-dense point exploded with an extraordinary force to create matter, pushing the latter outward to form billions of galaxies. Our galaxy, the Milky Way, is a drop in the Big Bang's Ocean. So, after the first supernova, all known matter existed. Stars, planets, moons, earth, and us.

Yes, we're made of the same ingredients as the stars. Read how fascinating the patterns found in nature are: How the death of a star resembles the birth of a cell, how the helix nebula is identical to the human eye, how the network of galaxies compares to the network of neurons, how the formation of the universe resembles the neurons' firing, how a spiral galaxy and a hurricane from space are alike, how blood vessels are related to the veins of tree's leaves, how the world, like our body, is composed of 70% water, and how we are made of gases and minerals similar to those in stars. Even our bodies are cleaned of salt through drinking water, just as rain washes the earth of salt and carries it to the sea.

Moreover, we were born from the womb of the first star, our true mother. Our stepmother is Earth; therefore, we may have been formed from different stars' supernovas. Even our right hand may have been created from a different star than our left hand. And like all stars, we will not die but rather transform, and our atoms will dance in the universe to form new matter, our children—children who could be anything.

Death is birth, and birth is death. We are not within the universe but a piece that completes what completes us.

Ancient philosophers used to ponder how something could have been made from nothing. But not so long ago, this theory was proven true: in the beginning, energy existed as photons of energy and light. Both types consisted of photons and anti-photons. The positive and negative energy photons eliminated themselves, while photons of light produced one positive photon out of the 100 billion photons that were eliminated.

That one 'miracle' transformed into matter and validated *Einstein's* $E=mc^2$ theory, eventually making existence possible. To this day, the universe is still expanding because of every one of the hundred billion photons created. Nevertheless, the creation of these photons also made the making of electrons possible, and the elimination of both positive and negative types of the latter created hot-radiation energy photons that cool and decrease the universe's density over time.

Scientists also recently discovered, after *Hubble's* telescope monitoring of the light spectrum that comes from the stars, that stars and planets are moving away from Earth and each other at a rate ranging from thousands of kilometers to the speed of light. This movement is expanding the universe. Fantastic, chemistry is beautiful...

"And the heaven We constructed with strength, and indeed, we are its expander." —*The Qur'an, verse (51:47).*
Hey, what? What was discussed before, and which is a recent discovery, was already known 1400 years ago when the Qur'an first appeared... It states that the heavens, the universe, are constantly expanding by an unknown force...

"I swear by the locations of the stars (and their falling). It is indeed a very great oath if you but knew." —*The Qur'an, verse (56:75).*

Breath-taking! In addition to the ever-expanding universe, it has recently been revealed that the reason why the Qur'an mentions 'the locations of stars' rather than just 'the stars' is because we humans do not see stars when we gaze at the night sky, but only the locations they passed by seconds ago. That's because for the universe to expand, the stars would have to move away from the earth and each other at a rate ranging from thousand kilometers to the speed of light... and the moment we try to see them, it will be too late because they will have moved. What we see are the lights that they emit just before moving. We can't see the stars themselves because we'd go blind if we did, which is impossible anyway.

All the above, from creation to expansion and what occurs throughout existence, was created with incredible precision. The Qur'an even mentions miraculous sayings that astonished scholars. How could one be aware of current discoveries over a thousand years ago without today's sciences and technologies? None of the creations could've known, but their creator could. There's indeed a very great and powerful one who created something out of nothing and controls this marvelous process.

Moreover, there will come a time when the universe's expansion will reach its limit because the density and temperature of the atoms that make up the world are decreasing in parallel. The universe's fabric will be torn apart, and the greatest supernova of all will occur; everything will be transformed. Ultimately, we, the stars, planets, and everything will explode, and our atoms will form new planets that will shape the hereafter. Our bodies, alive or dead, will follow.

According to quantum physics, *"a particle vibrating due to your sound when you speak can affect a molecule inside a star at the edge of the universe instantly; this phenomenon is known as quantum entanglement. The greatest illusion of this universe is the illusion of separation."*

Therefore, you begin to wonder if the timing of the birth and death of new stars is somehow related to the birth and death of humans. And perhaps if there's some spiritual connection between space and time. Maybe our atoms have homes out there that they need to return to at a particular time. After all, they're free and can roam wherever they wish.

So, where is their home? Do they even have one at all? Or will they take us here and there, break free from boundaries, dance among galaxies, reveal reality, and be happy till eternity?

Ultimately, our home could be everywhere, anywhere, or nowhere...

"You know that point in your life when you realize the house you grew up in isn't really your home anymore? All of a sudden, even though you have someplace where you put your shit, that idea of home is gone." —Garden State, 2004.

Let's go somewhere no one knows our names,
and live everywhere nature isn't tamed.
Let's not hide but dance in the rain,
and jump off the non-stop train.

We are here to dwell on the earth temporarily, and dwelling means settling by following our hearts. Our atoms were, are, and must always remain free. Who are they to tell us where and what our homes are? Everything is pre-determined, pre-formed, and predefined. Artificial borders and commercial establishments are weaving the entire earth. I'll tell you something:

Home is not a place; it's not a form either. Home is where your heart belongs... It's a sensation, a feeling for something generated

*"You are only free when you realize you belong no place—you
belong every place—no place at all. The price is high. The reward
is great,"—Maya Angelou told Bill Moyers in a 1973 interview.*

Don't be afraid... Just open your arms and let the winds of
change blow on you. Your roots are your desires and
dreams. They don't break but rather move. Every time a root
moves, you become lighter until you fly. That's when you'll
succeed, at last, when you dare. Follow your heart; it knows
the way.

Do not care about people's gossip and criticism. Do not
sacrifice any of your dreams for anything or anyone. Pray not
only through rituals and ceremonies but also and mainly
through adventure, experience, and love! You, your dreams,
are your king; let your soul burn only by passion, by love.

*"If something burns your soul with purpose and desire, it's your
duty to be reduced to ashes by it. Any other form of existence will
be yet another dull book in the library of life."—Charles Bukowski*

Then and only then, after you have honored your soul,
when you leave this world and travel to solve the astonishing
mystery of mysteries, and someone asks how you died, the
answer will proudly be:

"Tell me how he died."

"I will tell you how he lived..."—The Last Samurai, 2003.

Awake

"Time's up. I hope you've all come up with something interesting... Let's start with you."

"Yeah, the sea is stunning today, more than ever before... There is real comfort in its emptiness, for it consists of a boundless, ever-changing movement whose existence is unchained and follows a natural rhythm that echoes in eternity. This rhythmic movement adopts an equation formed by logic and emotions, which both define life's theatre. This equation is transmitted and woven by a needle of light into our sensual mechanism, a miraculous name by itself, and which includes this mixture within it since its inception, like fated freedom. It naturally masters the rhythm through its perfect flaws in a way that makes our vessels of stars harmonize, and the more we listen, the more we enjoy the song; the silent song... We can hear and understand it without a word. The emptiness of the sea may be silent, but its silence is not empty; It's full of answers and signs. But only those willing to listen can enjoy the music."

"This...is captivating, but I've been discussing your thesis. What is Architecture or home to you?"

"Exactly... Stare at how she beautifully stands in place, spreads her wings, anchors her bones with glowing skin and a mosaic of leaves, dances with the wind, kisses the sun, and plays with the rain. And when autumn arrives, she drops its heavy load and then grows back, welcoming change and life. And you're asking me why I love her? That's because I haven't fallen in love with her leaves. After that, I won't know what to do when autumn comes. I've fallen in love with her bones, with her roots. And this is the beauty of true love, the universe's love."

"Son, are you ... all there? Who are you?"

"Do you know that we're related? Seriously, I might even be older than you. Well, to answer your question..."

"I'm both something and nothing: Sometimes I wish who, ask when, and then wonder why. But other times, I wonder who, wish when, and then ask why. The only thing I know? Oh, it's 'what'."

"Fine, I suppose you haven't finished yet. Do you need more time?"

"How can I finish something unfinished and incomplete, of the same yet different space and time?"

"Well... so you don't have an answer yet?"

"Oh, on the contrary, I know exactly where my answer is; I just need to find it...

...Thank you, I feel much better.”

....

“I think that I need to stay longer in the light.”

....

“Of course, I forgot, you already know that...”

Browsing

As the journey nears its end, I'd like to highlight some notions:

The story begins and ends with a mysterious dialogue between two unknown parties where parentheses aren't closed or opened. How is that linked to the story?

The story begins with a chapter titled 'A Moment,' where two dialogues occur suddenly but with different interlocutors whose genders vary. Why?

Time is ambiguous throughout the story when/where the character suddenly speaks to others between chapters. Therefore, is the character experiencing events physically or mentally? Or perhaps both?

There are some grammar/vocabulary errors in the book. Are they mistakes or part of the writer's flaws? Or both?

The writer mentions events that occurred just before one died in the 'Perfect Flaws' chapter. How is this related to the story's quotes, both the writer's sayings and cited ones? What do the quotes represent?

The book first doubts science and religion but later trusts religion through science. Why?

The book argues about a secret organization. Research it to be 'Awake.'

The story concludes with a chapter titled 'Awake,' with all chapters' names mentioned in the dialogue between the interlocutors. Is that a coincidence? Are they all connected?

Love and Home are essential in the story. How are they related? Or are they the same for the character?

The sea was stated at the beginning and end of the book. What does it convey?

Is the answer of the character he seeks related to the cover page? And what are the beginning and the end for him?

Following the 'Dreamy Reality' chapter, are the character and the writer the same or different? Or maybe one is a reality, and the other is its copy? Is the entire story/book even real? And what is reality?

I leave it to my dear readers to experience and define these notions and the story's events based on their perspectives and souls. I give you my best regards and wish you all love.

Issam Raad, or not?